The Real Companion

Poetry and Prose in Praise of the Pint

Compiled by Hugh Morrison

Montpelier Publishing
London
MMXV

ISBN-13: 978-1507622704
ISBN-10: 1507622708
Published by Montpelier Publishing, London.
Printed by Amazon Createspace.
Cover image: Ian T/Geograph
This edition copyright © 2015. All rights reserved.

Introduction

Ale shall now engage my pen
To set at rest the hearts of men.

Walter de Biblesworth (13th century)

In 1971 four men sat in a pub bemoaning the terrible state of British beer. Industrialised brewing and pub chains, catering for the mass market, had reduced a once great drink to an insipid, chemical-laden alcohol delivery device. Where was the beer of old England, celebrated for centuries in drinking songs and poetry? What had happened to the craftsmanship and skill of the once great brewing trade?

They decided to do something about it and formed the Campaign for Real Ale (CAMRA). Since then CAMRA, now with over 150,000 members, has been at the forefront of a renaissance in British brewing, promoting high standards in traditionally made beer, or real ale. The change over the last four decades has been dramatic and has not been confined to the United Kingdom, with the trend for 'craft beers' spreading across the USA and in many other parts of the world.

It is high time, then, to revisit some of the great writing of the past which celebrated the grand old drink of beer. The editor has tapped the best barrels of the world's literary cellars to bring you a mouth watering collection of poems, songs and prose passages from the last five centuries in celebration of beer—the perfect companion to a pint of real ale.

So raise your glasses and drink deep.

The Editor.

Dost thou think, because thou art virtuous, there shall be no more cakes and ale?

Shakespeare

Old England's Good Cheer

Let us sing our own treasures, Old England's good cheer,
To the profits and pleasures of stout British beer;
Your wine tippling, dram sipping fellows retreat,
But your beer drinking Britons can never be beat.
The French with their vineyards and meagre pale ale,
They drink from the squeezing of half ripe fruit;
But we, who have hop-yards to mellow our ale,
Are rosy and plump and have freedom to boot.

Anon, c.1757

The Name of Beer

The name of Beer seems to have puzzled for a long time the ingenuity of scholars who attempted many etymological explanations, more or less probable. There is now no doubt that it is derived from the old Saxon word *bere*, which meant barley.

From On Beer *by M. Vogel (1874)*

Bottled Beer Begins with a Bang

Fuller, in his Worthies of England, ascribes the invention of bottled beer to Alexander Newell, Dean of St. Paul's and a master of

Westminster School in the reign of Queen Mary. The Dean was a devoted angler. 'But,' says old Fuller, 'whilst Newell was catching of fishes, Bishop Bonner was catching of Newell, and would certainly have sent him to the shambles, had not a good London merchant conveyed him away upon the seas.'

Newell was engaged in his favourite pursuit on the banks of the Thames, when such pressing notice of his danger reached him, that he was obliged to take immediate flight. On his return to England, after Mary's death, he remembered, when resuming his old amusement, that on the day of his flight he had left his simple repast, the liquor of which consisted of a bottle of beer, in a safe place in the river bank; there he sought it, and, as the quaint language of Fuller informs us, he 'found it no bottle, but a gun, such the sound at the opening thereof; and this is believed (casualty is the mother of more invention than industry) the original of bottled ale in England.'

From *The Curiosities of Ale and Beer* by John Bickerdyke (1889)

A Beer Drinker's Epitaph

Poor John Scott lies buried here;
Tho' once he was both hale and stout.
Death stretched him on his bitter bier:
In another world he hops about.

In a Bristol Tavern

Three jolly coachmen
sat in a Bristol Tavern,
and they decided,
to have another flagon.

Landlord fill the flowing bowl,
until it doth run over.
For tonight we'll merry, merry be.
Tomorrow we'll be sober.

Here's to the man who drinks small beer,
and goes to bed quite sober.
Fades as the leaves do fade,
and drop off in October.

Here's to the man who drinks strong ale,
and goes to bed quite mellow.
Lives as he ought to live,
and dies a jolly good fellow.

Here's to the girl who steals a kiss,
and runs to tell her mother.
She's a very foolish thing.
She'll never get another.

Here's to the girl who steals a kiss,
and runs back for another.
She's a boon to all mankind.
Very soon she'll be a mother.

If I had another brick,
I'd build by chimney higher.
It would stop my neighbour's cat,
from pissing on my fire.

Come, into the garden Maude,
and don't be so particular.
If the grass is cold and damp,
We'll do it perpendicular.

Landlord fill the flowing bowl,
until it doth run over.
For tonight we'll merry, merry be.
Tomorrow we're Hungover.

Anon

The Best Bass He Ever Drank

...the very best Bass I ever drank had had an exactly contrary experience. In the year 1875, when I was resident at Elgin, I and a friend now dead, the Procurator-Fiscal of the district, devoted the May 'Sacrament holidays,' which were then still kept in those remote parts, to a walking tour up the Findhorn and across to Loch Ness and Glen Urquhart.

At the Freeburn Inn on the first-named river we found some beer of singular excellence: and, asking the damsel who waited on us about it, were informed that a cask of Bass had been put in during the previous October, but, owing to a sudden break in the weather and the departure of all visitors, had never been tapped till our arrival.

From Beer and Cider *by George Saintsbury (1845-1933)*

I Like a Drop of Good Beer

Why, we'll smoke and drink our beer.
For I like a drop of good beer, I does.
I'ze fond of good beer, I is.
Let gentlemen fine sit down to their wine
But we'll all of us here stick to our beer.

Anon

The Beeriad, or Progress of Drink

The...occasion was the coming-of-age of the Marquis of Worcester (now the Duke of Beaufort). I had to get to Badminton House by road, and engaged a gig for the journey. On arrival I was handed over to the care of the butler, and after a look round the grounds, where an ox was being roasted and village sports were in progress, was taken into a comfortable room and regaled with cold boiled beef and ale.

And then my good friend the butler produced a jug of something special which he poured into a tall, narrow glass with as much care as if it had been 1820 brandy or '34 port. It was ale that had been brewed when the Marquis was born, and was consequently twenty-one years old. Nothing could have been nicer. Soft and silky, with a nutty flavour, it slipped down as easily as milk, and did not seem as if it were a bit stronger.

I ought to have been warned. Perhaps I was warned and ignored the warning. Anyhow, I drank two full glasses, and then — a blank. What happened, I do not know, but probably I fell into a deep sleep. Late in the evening I recovered enough to get into the gig and start for Bristol. All I can say is that the horse did the rest.

From Chestnuts and Small Beer *by Henry James Jennings*

The Empty Bottle

Ah, liberty! how like thou art
To this large bottle lying here,
Which yesterday from foreign mart,
Came filled with potent English beer!
A touch of steel—a hand—a gush—
A pop that sounded far and near—
A wild emotion—liquid rush—
And I had drunk that English beer!
And what remains—An empty shell!
A lifeless form both sad and queer,
A temple where no god doth dwell—
The simple memory of beer!

William Aytoun (1813-1865)

Hermit Hoar

Hermit hoar, in solemn cell,
Wearing out life's evening gray;
Smite thy bosom, sage, and tell,
What is bliss, and which the way?
Thus I spoke; and speaking sigh'd;
Scarce repressed a starting tear;
When the smiling sage reply'd
Come, my lad, and drink some beer.

Dr Samuel Johnson (1709-1784)

Epitaph on John Dove, Innkeeper

Here lies Johnnie Pigeon;
What was his religion?
Whae'er desires to ken,
To some other warl'
Maun follow the carl,
For here Johnie Pigeon had nane!

Strong ale was ablution,
Small beer persecution,
A dram was *memento mori*;
But a full-flowing bowl
Was the saving his soul,
And port was celestial glory.

Robert Burns (1759-1796)

Beer

Here,
With my beer
I sit,
While golden moments flit:
Alas!

They pass
Unheeded by:
And, as they fly,
I,
Being dry,
Sit, idly sipping here
My beer.
O, finer far
Than fame, or riches, are
The graceful smoke-wreaths of this free cigar!

Why
Should I
Weep, wail, or sigh?
What if luck has passed me by?
What if my hopes are dead,—
My pleasures fled?
Have I not still
My fill
Of right good cheer,—
Cigars and beer?
Go, whining youth,
Forsooth!
Go, weep and wail,
Sigh and grow pale,

Weave melancholy rhymes
On the old times,
Whose joys like shadowy ghosts appear,
But leave to me my beer!
Gold is dross,—
Love is loss,—
So, if I gulp my sorrows down,
Or see them drown
In foamy draughts of old nut-brown,
Then do I wear the crown,
Without the cross!

George Arnold (1834-1865)

Brawn of England's Lay

The villeins clustered round the bowl
At merrie Yule to make good cheer,
And drank with froth on beard and jowl:
'Was-hael to the Thane!
May never Breton taste our beer,
Nor Dane.'

Till the red cock on the chimney crew,
And each man cried with a mighty yawn
As the tapster one more flagon drew:
'To the Saxon land was-hael!
May we never want for mast-fed brawn
Nor ale!'

The thane took up the stirrup-cup
And blew off the reaming head,
And at one draught he swigged it up
And smacked his lips and said:
'Was-hael to coulter and sword!
Was-hael to hearth and hall!
To Saxon land and Saxon lord
And thrall.'

John Hunter-Duvar (1821-1899)

Wed

For these white arms about my neck—
For the dainty room, with its ordered grace—
For my snowy linen without a fleck—
For the tender charm of this uplift face—

For the softened light and the homelike air—
The low luxurious cannel fire—
The padded ease of my chosen chair—
The devoted love that discounts desire—

I sometimes think, when Twelve is struck
By the clock on the mantel, tinkling clear,
I would take—and thank the gods for the luck—
One single hour with the boys and the beer.

Where the sawdust scent of a cheap saloon
Is mingled with malt; where each man smokes,
Where they sing the street songs out of tune,
Talk Art, and bandy ephemeral jokes.

By Jove, I do! And all the time
I know not a man that is there to-night
But would barter his brains to be where I'm—
And I'm well aware that the beggars are right.

Henry Cuyler Bunner (1855-1896)

Guid Ale Keeps the Heart Aboon

Chorus—O gude ale comes and gude ale goes;
Gude ale gars me sell my hose,
Sell my hose, and pawn my shoon—
Gude ale keeps my heart aboon!

I had sax owsen in a pleugh,
And they drew a' weel eneugh:
I sell'd them a' just ane by ane—
Gude ale keeps the heart aboon!

O gude ale comes, &c.

Gude ale hauds me bare and busy,
Gars me moop wi' the servant hizzie,
Stand i' the stool when I hae done—
Gude ale keeps the heart aboon!

Robert Burns (1759-1796)

Heather Ale: a Galloway Legend

From the bonny bells of heather
They brewed a drink long-syne,
Was sweeter far than honey,
Was stronger far than wine.

They brewed it and they drank it,
And lay in a blessed swound
For days and days together
In their dwellings underground.

There rose a king in Scotland,
A fell man to his foes,
He smote the Picts in battle,
He hunted them like roes.

Over miles of the red mountain
He hunted as they fled,
And strewed the dwarfish bodies
Of the dying and the dead.

Summer came in the country,
Red was the heather bell;
But the manner of the brewing
Was none alive to tell.

In graves that were like children'
On many a mountain head,
The Brewsters of the Heather
Lay numbered with the dead.

The king in the red moorland
Rode on a summer's day;
And the bees hummed, and the curlews
Cried beside the way.

The king rode, and was angry;
Black was his brow and pale,
To rule in a land of heather
And lack the Heather Ale.

It fortuned that his vassals,
Riding free on the heath,
Came on a stone that was fallen
And vermin hid beneath.

Rudely plucked from their hiding,
Never a word they spoke:
A son and his aged father—
Last of the dwarfish folk.

The king sat high on his charger,
He looked on the little men;
And the dwarfish and swarthy couple
Looked at the king again.

Down by the shore he had them;
And there on the giddy brink—
'I will give you life, ye vermin,
For the secret of the drink.'

There stood the son and father
And they looked high and low;
The heather was red around them,
The sea rumbled below.

And up and spoke the father,
Shrill was his voice to hear:
'I have a word in private,
A word for the royal ear.

'Life is dear to the aged,
And honour a little thing;
I would gladly sell the secret,'
Quoth the Pict to the King.

His voice was small as a sparrow's,
And shrill and wonderful clear:
'I would gladly sell my secret,
Only my son I fear.'

'For life is a little matter,
And death is nought to the young;
And I dare not sell my honour
Under the eye of my son.

'Take him, O king, and bind him,
And cast him far in the deep;
And it's I will tell the secret
That I have sworn to keep.'

They took the son and bound him,
Neck and heels in a thong,
And a lad took him and swung him,
And flung him far and strong,

And the sea swallowed his body,
Like that of a child of ten;—
And there on the cliff stood the father,
Last of the dwarfish men.

'True was the word I told you:
Only my son I feared;
For I doubt the sapling courage
That goes without the beard.

But now in vain is the torture,
Fire shall never avail:
Here dies in my bosom
The secret of Heather Ale.'

Robert Louis Stevenson (1850-94)

From The Ballad of Lager Bier

In fallow college days, Tom Harland,
We both have known the ways of Yale,
And talked of many a nigh and far land,
O'er many a famous tap of ale.

There still they sing their *Gaudeamus*,
And see the road to glory clear;
But taps, that in our day were famous,
Have given place to Lager Bier.

Now, settled in this island-city,
We let new fashions have their weight;
Though none too lucky—more's the pity!—
Can still beguile our humble state

By finding time to come together,
In every season of the year,
In sunny, wet, or windy weather,
And clink our mugs of Lager Bier.

On winter evenings, cold and blowing,
'T is good to order ''alf and 'alf';
To watch the fire-lit pewter glowing,
And laugh a hearty English laugh;

Or even a sip of mountain whiskey
Can raise a hundred phantoms dear
Of days when boyish blood was frisky,
And no one heard of Lager Bier.

Yet of all bibulous compoundings,
Extracts or brewings, mixed or clear,
The best, in substance and surroundings,
For frequent use, is Lager Bier.

Go, flaxen-haired and blue-eyed maiden,
My German Hebe! hasten through

You smoke-cloud, and return thou laden
With bread and cheese and bier for two.

Ah, yes! the Schweitzer hath a savour
Of marjoram and mountain thyme,
An odoriferous, Alpine flavour;
You almost hear the cow-bells chime

While eating it, or, dying faintly,
The Ranz-des-vaches entrance the ear,
Until you feel quite Swiss and saintly,
Above your glass of Lager Bier.

Here come our drink, froth-crowned and sunlit,
In goblets with high-curving arms,
Drawn from a newly opened runlet,
As bier must be, to have its charms,

This primal portion each shall swallow
At one draught, for a pioneer;
And thus a ritual usage follow
Of all who honour Lager Bier.

Glass after glass in due succession,
Till, borne through midriff, heart and brain,
He mounts his throne and takes possession,—
The genial Spirit of the grain!

Edmund Clarence Stedman (1833-1906)

The Robust Drinkers of Cambridge

Very strong beer permits itself, of course, to be bottled and kept in bottles: but I rather doubt whether it also is not best from the wood; though it is equally of course, much easier to cellar it and keep it bottled. Its kinds are various and curious. 'Scotch ale' is famous, and at its best (I never drank better than Younger's) excellent: but its tendency, I think, is to be too sweet.

I once invested in some—not Younger's—which I kept for nearly sixteen years, and which was still treacle at the end. Bass's No. 1 requires no praises. Once when living in the Cambridgeshire village mentioned earlier I had some, bottled in Cambridge itself, of great age and excellence. Indeed, two guests, though both of them were Cambridge men, and should have had what Mr. Lang once called the 'robust' habits of that University, fell into one ditch after partaking of it. (I own that the lanes thereabouts are very dark.)

From Beer and Cider *by George Saintsbury (1845-1933)*

Lady Onlie, Honest Luckie

A' the lads o' Thorniebank,
When they gae to the shore o' Bucky,
They'll step in an' tak a pint
Wi' Lady Onlie, honest Lucky.

Chorus.—Lady Onlie, honest Lucky,
Brews gude ale at shore o' Bucky;
I wish her sale for her gude ale,
The best on a' the shore o' Bucky.

Her house sae bien, her curch sae clean
I wat she is a daintie chuckie;
And cheery blinks the ingle-gleed
O' Lady Onlie, honest Lucky!

Lady Onlie, &c.

Robert Burns (1756-1799)

The Nut-Brown Ale

The nut-brown ale, the nut-brown ale,
Puts down all drink when it is stale!
The toast, the nutmeg, and the ginger
Will make a sighing man a singer.

Ale gives a buffet in the head,
But ginger under-props the brain;
When ale would strike a strong man dead
Then nutmeg tempers it again.

The nut-brown ale, the nut-brown ale,
Puts down all drink when it is stale!
The Sheriffe of Oxford late is grown so wise
As to reprieve his Beere till next assize:

Alas! 'twas not so quick, 'twas not so heady,
The Jury sate and found it dead already.

William Strode (1602-1644)

Church Ale

Church ale was so called from being used at the feasts celebrated in commemoration of the consecration of a church. The congregation elected two heralds, who had to go round and make collections in the village. With the amount thus received they bought pastry and drinkables, which were consumed at Whitsuntide.

At some places they bought malt from parish funds and voluntary contributions, and made a quantity of strong beer of it, that was sold partly in the church and partly at other places for the benefit of the church.

From On Beer *by M. Vogel (1874)*

From Pipes and Beer

Before I was famous I used to sit
In a dull old under-ground room I knew,
And sip cheap beer, and be glad for it,
With a wild Bohemian friend or two.

And oh, it was joy to loiter thus,
At peace in the heart of the city's stir,
Entombed, while life hurried over us,
In our lazy bacchanal sepulchre.

The Teuton beer-bibbers came and went,
Night after night, and stared, good folk,
At our table, noisy with argument,
And our chronic aureoles of smoke.

And oh, my life! but we all loved well
The talk,—free, fearless, keen, profound,—
The rockets of wit that flashed and fell
In that dull old tavern under-ground!

But there came a change in my days at last,
And fortune forgot to starve and stint,
And the people chose to admire aghast
The book I had eaten dirt to print.

And new friends gathered about me then,
New voices summoned me there and here;
The world went down in my dingy den,
And drew me forth from the pipes and beer.

I took the stamp of my altered lot,
As the sands of the certain seasons ran,
And slowly, whether I would or not,
I felt myself growing a gentleman.

But now and then I would break the thrall,
I would yield to a pang of dumb regret,
And steal to join them, and find them all,
With the amber wassail near them yet,—

So they waned and waned, these visits of mine,
'Till I married the heiress, ending here.
For if caste approves the cigars and wine,
She must frown perforce upon pipes and beer.

And now 'tis years since I saw these men,
Years since I knew them living yet.
And of this alone I am sure since then,—
That none has gained what he toiled to get.

Well, and what has it all been worth?
May not my soul to my soul confess
That 'succeeding,' here upon earth,
Does not alway assume success?

I would cast, and gladly, from this gray head
Its crown, to regain one sweet lost year
With artist George, with splenetic Fred,
With dreamy Frank, with the pipes and beer!

Edgar Fawcett (1847-1904)

Beers of Elizabethan England

...there is such heady ale and beer in most of them as for the mightiness thereof among such as seek it out is commonly called 'huffcap,' 'the mad dog,' 'Father Whoreson,' 'angels' food' 'dragon's milk,' 'go-by-the-wall,' 'stride wide,' and 'lift leg,' etc.

And this is more to be noted, that when one of late fell by God's providence into a troubled conscience, after he had considered well of his reachless life and dangerous estate, another, thinking belike to change his colour and not his mind, carried him straight away to the strongest ale, as to the next physician.

It is incredible to say how our maltbugs lug at this liquor, even as pigs should lie in a row lugging at their dame's teats, till they lie still again and be not able to wag. Neither did Romulus and Remus suck their she-wolf or shepherd's wife Lupa with such eager and sharp devotion as these men hale at 'huffcap,' till they be red as cocks and little wiser than their combs.

From A Description of Elizabethan England *by William Harrison*

From John Barleycorn

John Barleycorn was a hero bold,
Of noble enterprise;
For if you do but taste his blood,
'Twill make your courage rise.
'Twill make a man forget his woe;
'Twill heighten all his joy;
'Twill make the widow's heart to sing,
Tho' the tear were in her eye.
Then let us toast John Barleycorn,
Each man a glass in hand;
And may his great posterity
Ne'er fail in old Scotland!

Robert Burns (1759-1796)

The Noble Liquor Called Guinness

The comeliest of black malts is, of course, that noble liquor called of Guinness. Here at least I think England cannot match Ireland, for our stouts are, as a rule, too sweet and 'clammy.' But there used to be in the country districts a sort of light porter which was one of the most refreshing liquids conceivable for hot weather. I have drunk it in

Yorkshire at the foot of Roseberry Topping, out of big stone bottles like champagne magnums. But that was nearly sixty years ago.

From Beer and Cider *by George Saintsbury (1845-1933)*

Lines on Ale

Fill with mingled cream and amber,
I will drain that glass again.
Such hilarious visions clamber
Through the chamber of my brain.
Quaintest thoughts, queerest fancies
Come to life and fade away.
What care I how time advances;
I am drinking ale today.

Edgar Allen Poe (1809-1849)

The Ale of the Ancient Britons

It would appear, however, that ale, which certainly was the ale of the ancient Britons, was not brewed with hops until about the year 1730, and from about the same period dates also the invention of porter.

It was invented by a brewer named Harwood, and, being mostly consumed by porters, obtained therefrom the name of porter. It was made of two kinds, single and double porter (brown stout), the latter containing of course more malt than the former.

From On Beer *by M. Vogel (1874)*

Jolly Good Ale and Old

I cannot eat but little meat,—
My stomach is not good;
But, sure, I think that I can drink
With him that wears a hood.

Though I go bare, take ye no care;
I nothing am a-cold,—
I stuff my skin so full within
Of jolly good ale and old.

Back and side go bare, go bare;
Both foot and hand go cold;
But, belly, God send thee good ale enough,
Whether it be new or old!

I love no roast but a nut-brown toast,
And a crab laid in the fire;
A little bread shall do me stead,—
Much bread I not desire.

No frost, nor snow, nor wind, I trow,
Can hurt me if I wold,—
I am so wrapt, and thorowly lapt
Of jolly good ale and old.

And Tyb, my wife, that as her life
Loveth well good ale to seek,
Full oft drinks she, till you may see
The tears run down her cheek;

Then doth she trowl to me the bowl,
Even as a malt-worm should;
And saith, 'Sweetheart, I took my part
Of this jolly good ale and old.'

Now let them drink till they nod and wink,
Even as good fellows should do;
They shall not miss to have the bliss
Good ale doth bring men to;

And all poor souls that have scoured bowls,
Or have them lustily trowled,
God save the lives of them and their wives,
Whether they be young or old!

Back and side go bare, go bare;
Both foot and hand go cold;
But, belly, God send thee good ale enough,
Whether it be new or old!

William Stevenson (1530?-1575)

The Champagne of Beers

In former days, though probably not at present, you could often find rather choice specimens of strong beer produced at small breweries in the country. I remember such even in the Channel Islands.

And I suspect the Universities themselves have been subject to 'declensions and fallings off.' I know that in my undergraduate days at Merton we always had proper beer-glasses, like the old 'flute' champagnes, served regularly at cheese-time with a most noble beer called 'Archdeacon,' which was then actually brewed in the sacristy of the College chapel.

From Beer and Cider *by George Saintsbury (1845-1933)*

From The Hour Before Dawn

A great lad with a beery face
Had tucked himself away beside
A ladle and a tub of beer,
And snored, no phantom by his look.
So with a laugh at his own fear
He crawled into that pleasant nook.
'Night grows uneasy near the dawn
Till even I sleep light; but who
Has tired of his own company?
What one of Maeve's nine brawling sons
Sick of his grave has wakened me?
But let him keep his grave for once
That I may find the sleep I have lost.'
What care I if you sleep or wake?

But I'll have no man call me ghost.'
Say what you please, but from daybreak
I'll sleep another century.'
And I will talk before I sleep
And drink before I talk.'
And he
Had dipped the wooden ladle deep
Into the sleeper's tub of beer
Had not the sleeper started up.
Before you have dipped it in the beer
I dragged from Goban's mountain-top
I'll have assurance that you are able
To value beer; no half-legged fool
Shall dip his nose into my ladle
Merely for stumbling on this hole
In the bad hour before the dawn.'
Why beer is only beer.'

William Butler Yeats (1865-1939)

Unhopped Beer

The old Anglo-Saxons drank unhopped beer, as is gathered from its being mentioned in the laws of Ina, King of Essex. Mention is likewise made of beer in the description of a feast given by Edward the Confessor, and at the time of the Normans it was so cheap that two gallons cost only one penny. Afterwards hops were also cultivated in England, and must have been known at an early period, for otherwise Henry IV (1400) and Henry VI could not have prohibited their cultivation.

From On Beer *by M. Vogel (1874)*

When Wine Took Over

In Holinshed's time (about 1570) different descriptions of beer were brewed in England. The best was called March beer, because it was brewed in March, and it was commonly drunk after being one month old, but at the tables of distinguished people, one and two years old. From that time, wine, which was imported in many qualities, superseded beer-drinking.

From On Beer *by M. Vogel (1874)*

The Ale of Trinity College, Cambridge

I have a friend who loveth me
And sendeth me Ale of Trinitie
A very good fellow is my true friend
With talents and virtues without end

Filled with Learning's very best seed
Ready to think or drink at need
In short a very good fellow indeed

But the best of all is as it seems to me
That he yieldeth the Ale of Trinitie.

Oh Trinitie Ale is stout and good
Whether in bottle it be or wood
'Tis good at morning tis good at night
Ye should drink whilst the liquor is bubbling bright

Tis good for man and woman and child
Being neither too strong nor yet too mild
It strengthens the body it strengthens the mind
And hitteth the toper's taste refined.

Ale! Ale! if properly understood
Promoteth a brotherly neighbourhood

Now what can be better on winter night
When the fagot is blazing bright

And your friend is perplex'd how to kill the time
With Useful Knowledge or idle rhyme
To step in and say Neighbour I think
Your Trinitie ale must be fit to drink

'Let's try it.' He answers 'With all my soul'
And in the capacious tumblers roll
Hark to the music rich and rare
Note how it stealeth the sting from Care

Behold both Pride and Prudery bend
And each man groweth a warmer friend.

Anon, from Colburn's New Monthly Magazine and Humorist *(1842).*

Better than Medicine

A glass of bitter beer or pale ale, taken with the principal meal of the day, does more good, and less harm, than any medicine the physician can prescribe.

Dr Carpenter in The Scottish Review, *(1750)*

In Search of Real Lager

Genuine lager beer is no more to be boycotted than genuine hock, though, by the way, the best that I ever drank (it was at the good town of King's Lynn) was Low not High Dutch in origin. It was so good that I wrote to the shippers at Rotterdam to see if I could get some sent to Leith, but the usual difficulties in establishing connection between wholesale dealers and individual buyers prevented this.

From *Beer and Cider* by George Saintsbury (1845-1933)

A Glass of Old Burton

The doctors may boast of their lotions,
Old women delight in their tea;
But I scorn all such rubbishing potions:
A glass of old Burton for me!

Let the faculty sneer as it pleases
My recipe can never fail
The Nepenthe that cures all diseases
Is a bumper of Allsopp's* ale.

Anon

Samuel Allsopp and Sons of Burton on Trent, later part of the Ind Coope group

Dear Beer

Beer-drinking remained a family custom in England, with high and low, up to the fourteenth century; but about the year 1307 beer had become dearer, and its price according to quality was two, three, or four pence a gallon. Accordingly, a regulation of the Corporation of the city of London determined that a gallon of best beer should only cost three half-pence and common beer one penny.

From On Beer *by M. Vogel (1874)*

In Praise of Ale

Ale is rightly called nappy, for it will set a nap upon a mans threadbare eyes when he is sleepy.

It is called Merry-goe-downe, for it slides downe merrily; It is fragrant to the Scent. It is most pleasing to the taste. The flowring and mantling of it. (like chequer worke) with verdant smiling of it, it is delightefull to the Sight, it is Touching or Feeling to the Braine and Heart; and (to please the senses all) it provokes men to singing and mirth, which is contenting to the Hearing.

The speedy taking of it doth comfort a heavy troubled minde; it will make a weeping widowe laugh and forget sorrow for her deceas'd husband. It will set a Bashfull Suiter a wooing; It heates the chill blood of Aged; it will cause a man to speake past his owne or any other man's capacity, or understanding; It sets an Edge on Logick and Rhetorick; It is a friend to the Muses; It inspires the poore Poet, that cannot compasse the price of Canarie or Gacoign; It mounts the Musican 'bove Eccla;

It makes the Balladmaker Rime beyond Reason; It is a Repairer of a decaide Colour in the face; It puts Eloquence into the Oratour; It will make the Philosopher talke profoundly, the Scholar learnedly, and the Lawyer acute and feelingly.

Ale at Whitesontide, or at Whitsontide or a Whitson Church Ale, is a repairer of decayed Countrey Churches; It is a great friend to Truth; so they that drinke of it (to the purpose) will reveale all they know, be it never so secret to be kept;

It is a Embleme of Justice, for it allowes, and veeds measure; It will put courage into a Coward, and make him swagger and fight; It is a Seale to many a good Bargaine. The Physittian will commend it; the Lawyer will defend it; It neither hurts or kils any but those that abuse it unmeasurably and beyond bearing;

It doth good to as many as take it rightly; It is as good as a Paire of Spectacles to clear the Eyesight of an Old Parish Clarke; and in Conclusion, it is such a nourisher of Mankinde, that if my Mouth were as bigge as Bishopgaet, my Pen as long as a Maypole, and my Inke a flowing spring, or a standing fishpond yet I could not with my Mouth, Pen or Inke speake or write the truw worth and worthiness of Ale.

John Taylor, 'The Water Poet' (1580-1653)

Excerpt from A Shropshire Lad

Why, if 'tis dancing you would be,
There's brisker pipes than poetry.
Say, for what were hop-yards meant,
Or why was Burton built on Trent?
Oh many a peer of England brews
Livelier liquor than the Muse,
And malt does more than Milton can
To justify God's ways to man.
Ale, man, ale's the stuff to drink
For fellows whom it hurts to think:
Look into the pewter pot
To see the world as the world's not.
And faith, 'tis pleasant till 'tis past:
The mischief is that 'twill not last.
Oh I have been to Ludlow fair
And left my necktie God knows where,
And carried half way home, or near,
Pints and quarts of Ludlow beer:
Then the world seemed none so bad,
And I myself a sterling lad;
And down in lovely muck I've lain,
Happy till I woke again.
Then I saw the morning sky:
Heigho, the tale was all a lie;
The world, it was the old world yet,
I was I, my things were wet,
And nothing now remained to do
But begin the game anew.

A.E. Housman (1859-1936)

Ale's a Physician

Submit, bunch of grapes to the strong barley ear;
The weak wine no longer the laurel shall wear.
Sack, and all drinks else, desist from the strife—
Ale's the true *aquavitae* and liquor of life.

Then come, my boon fellows, let's drink it around;
It keeps us from grave, though it lays us on ground.

Ale's a physician; no mountebank bragger;
Can cure the chill ague, though it be with the stagger.
Ale's a strong wrestler—flings all it hath met;
And makes the ground slippery, though it be not wet.

Ale is both Ceres and good Neptune too;
Ale's froth was the sea from which Venus grew.
Ale is immortal; and be there no stops
In bonny lads quaffing, can live without hops.

Then come, my boon fellows, let's drink it around;
It keeps us from grave, though it lays us on ground.

Anon, from The London Chanticleers *(1659)*

It's Hard to Get at Good Beer

'Landlord!' says I,
With a face all wry,
'What do you call this here?'

'Gents,' says he,
'It's a pot of what we
Serve out as very best beer.
But it's hard to get at good beer,
For the brewer sells it so dear;
And the rents is so high,

'That' – 'in fact,' says I,
'You rob a poor man of his beer.'

Anon.

How India Pale Ale (IPA) was born

It happened at this time *(1822)*, that dining with an East Indian Director, Mr. Marjoribanks, in the course of conversation *(Samuel Allsopp)* happened to make some remark on the late occurrences in Russia, the neglect of his remonstrances by the government, and the gloomy prospects of his house from the loss of their European trade.

'But why not, Allsopp,' observed Mr. Marjoribanks, 'leave the cold climates, and try the warmer regions of the earth? Why do you not make an attempt on the Indian market?'

'I never heard of it.'

'There are 5,000 hogsheads of English beer sent to Madras and Bengal every year; and, what is more to your purpose, it is a trade that can never be lost; for the climate is too hot for brewing, unless at a distance so great that the carriage must eat up all the profits; and no tariff can ever affect you. We are all now dependent upon Hodgson, who has given offence to most of our merchants in India. But your Burton ale, so strong and sweet, will not suit our market.'

Here Mr. Marjoribanks rang the bell, and directed his butler to bring in a bottle of Hodgson's ale, that had been to India and back. The butler poured out a glass for Mr. Allsopp, who held it up to the light, and then, tasting it, exclaimed, 'Is this the Indian Beer? I can brew it.'

'If you can, it will be a fortune to you,' was Mr. Marjoribank's reply.

On Mr. Allsopp's return to Burton-on-Trent, sitting one morning in his counting-house, one of the men came to tell him, 'There's a hamper for you, sir, just come down by the mail from London.'

On opening this it was found to contain a dozen of ale; and with some joke about 'coals to Newcastle' 'a present of ale to Samuel Allsopp at Burton!' — he took up a bottle on which was written 'Hodgson's Indian beer.' Little did Mr. Allsopp imagine that he had at that moment in his hand the key to a colossal business, and the foundation of the future great prosperity of Burton-upon-Trent.

From Burton and its Bitter Beer *by J Stevenson Bushnan. (1853)*

Epitaph

Thomas Thomson's buried here
And what is more, he's in his bier
In life thy beer did thee surround
And now with thee is in the ground.

Cool Britannia

What two ideas are more inseparable than Beer and Britannia?

Rev Sydney Smith (1771-1845)

Brasenose Ale

O ale! *aurum potabile!*
That gildest life's dull hours,
When its colour weareth shabbily,
When fade its summer flowers.

Anon

Cooled in the Flowing River

Oh my beloved brother of the rod, do you know the taste of beer—of bitter beer—cooled in the flowing river? Not you; I warrant...Take, then, your bottle of beer, sink it deep, deep in the shady water, where the cooling springs and freshes are. Then, the day being very hot and bright, and the sun blazing upon your devoted head, consider it a matter of duty to have to fish that long, wide stream.

An hour and a half or so, good hard hammering will bring you to the end of it, and then—let me ask you *avec impressement*—how about that beer? Is it cool? Is it refreshing? Does it 'gurgle, gurgle, and go down glug,' as they say in Devonshire ? Is it heavenly? is it Paradise, and all the Peris to boot ? Ah! If you have never tasted beer under these, or similar circumstances, you have, believe me, never tasted it at all.

From By Lake and River *by Francis Francis, (1874)*

From A Panygeric on Oxford Ale

Balm of my cares, sweet solace of my toils,
Hail, Juice benignant! O'er the costly cups
Of riot-stirring wine, unwholesome draught.
Let Pride's loose sons prolong the wasteful night;
My sober evening let the tankard bless.
With toast embrown'd, and fragrant nutmeg fraught,
While the rich draught with oft repeated whiffs
Tobacco mild improves. Divine repast!
Where no crude surfeit, or intemperate joys
Of lawless Bacchus reigns ; but o'er my soul
A calm Lethean creeps; in drowsy trance
Each thought subsides, and sweet oblivion wraps
My peaceful brain, as if the leaden rod
Of magic Morpheus o'er mine eyes had shed
Its opiate influence. What though sore ills

Oppress, dire want of chill-dispelling coals.
Or cheerful candle (save the makeweight's gleam
Haply remaining), heart-rejoicing Ale
Cheers the sad scene, and every want supplies.

Thomas Warton, Poet Laureate (1728-1790)

Toper, Drink and Help the House

Toper, drink, and help the house—
Drink to every honest fellow;
Life was never worth a louse
To the man who ne'er was mellow.

How it sparkles! Here it goes!
Ale can make a blockhead shine;
Toper, torchlike may thy nose
Light thy face up, just like mine.

See old Sol, I like his notion.
With his whiskers all so red;
Sipping, drinking from the ocean,
Boozing till he goes to bed.

Yet poor beverage to regale!
Simple stuff to help his race—
Could he turn the sea to Ale,
How 'twould make him mend his pace!

Peter Pindar (John Wolcot). (1738-1819)

Beer! Happy Produce of our Isle

Beer! Happy produce of our isle,
Can sinewy strength impart.
And wearied with fatigue and toil,
Can cheer each manly heart.

Labour and art upheld by thee,
Successfully advance.
We quaff thy balmy juice with glee;
And water leave to France.

Genius of Health! Thy grateful taste
Rivals the cup of Jove,
And warms each English generous breast
With liberty and love.

James Towneley (1714-1778)

He that buys land buys many stones,
He that buys flesh buys many bones,
He, that buys eggs buys many shells,
But he that buys good ale buys nothing else.

Anon

To All Tapsters and Tipplers

To all tapsters and tipplers,
And all ale-house victualers,
Inn-keepers and cooks,
That for pot-sale looks,
And will not give measure,
But at your own pleasure,
Contrary to law,

Scant measure will draw
In pot and in can.
To cozen a man
Of his full quart a penny,
Of you there's too many.
For in King Harry's time,
When I made this rime
Of Elynor Rumming,
With her good ale tunning,
Our pots were full quarted,
We were not thus thwarted
With froth can and neck pot
And such nimble quick shot,
That a dozen will score
For twelve pints and no more.

Anon

Hell for Short Measure

The first ale-wife deserving of special mention is the Chester 'tapstere,' whose evil doings and fate are recorded in one of the Chester Misteries, or Miracle Plays, of the fourteenth century. The good folk of Chester seem to have had a peculiar dislike to being subjected to the tricks of dishonest brewers and taverners. Even in Saxon times it was a regulation of the City that one who brewed bad ale should be placed on a ducking-stool and plunged in a pool of muddy water. For the ale-wife of the old play a worse fate was reserved, and though she was a fictitious person, many of the audience would no doubt find little difficulty in fitting some of their acquaintances with the character depicted.

With that mixture of the sacred and profane which to a modern ear is, to say the least, somewhat startling, the Mystery in question describes the descent of Christ into Hell and the final redemption of all men out of purgatory – all, save one. A criminal remains whose sins are of so deep a dye that she may not be forgiven. She thus confesses her guilt:—

Some time I was a tavernere,
A gentel gossepp, and a tapstere
Of wine and ale, a trusty brewer,
Which woe hath me bewrought.
Of Cannes I kept no true measure.
My cuppes I solde at my pleasure,
Deceavinge many a creature,
Tho' my ale were nought.

The ale-wife is then carried off into Hell's mouth by the attendant demons, and the play closes.

From The Curiosities of Ale and Beer *by John Bidkerdyke (1889)*

For Now Our Land is Overflowne with Wine

For now our Land is overflowne with Wine:
With such a Deluge, or an Inundation
As hath besotted and halfe drown'd our Nation.
Some there are scarce worth 40 pence a yeere
Will hardly make a meale with Ale or Beere:
And will discourse, that wine doth make good blood,
Concocts his meat, and make digestion good,
And after to drink Beere, nor will, nor can
He lay a churl upon a Gentleman.

John Taylor, 'The Water Poet' (1578-1653)

Deceitful Wine

Deceitful wine! Embrew'd with mixtures dire,
By the curs'd vintner's art for sordid pelf.
O! Grant me, Heav'n, to live with health and ease,
My books, a sober friend. Small Beer, and sense:

So shall my years the smiling fates prolong,
And each auspicious morn shall see me happy.

Anon, from The Gentleman's Magazine, *(1746)*

Lager: Pride Comes Before a Fall

Lager beer is not unknown in England, and is sold at restaurants and hotels in most of our large towns. Much of it is imported; the rest comes from Lager-beer brewers, who have, within the last few years, started business in this country. Neither German nor Anglo-German beers appear to make much headway over here, nor is this very surprising when we remember how far superior our own ales and beers are to any brewed in Germany.

From *The Curiosities of Ale and Beer* by John Bickerdyke (1889)

Burton Ale

Ne'er tell me of liquors from Spain or from France,
They may get in your heels and inspire you to dance,
But the Ale of Old Burton if mellow and right
Will get in your head and inspire you to fight*.

Your Claret and Rhenish and fine Calcavella
Were never yet able to make a good fellow.
But of stout Burton Ale, if you drink but enough,
'Twill make you all jolly and hearty and tough.

Then let meagre Frenchmen still batten on Wine,
They ne'er will digest a good English Sirloin,
Parbleu they may caper and Vapour along,
But right Burton can make us both valiant and strong.

Come here then ye Mortals who're prone to despair
From frowns of Dame Fortune or frowns of the fair,

Whate'er your disorder, three nips will prevail,
And the best Panacea you'll find: Burton Ale.

Anon, from The London Magazine *(1784)*

*Presumably in battle, rather than in pub brawls.

Trinity College Ale

Oh, in truth, it gladdens the heart to see
What may spring from the Ale of Trinity,—
A scholar—a fellow,—a rector blithe,
(Fit to take any amount of tithe)—
Perhaps a bishop — perhaps, by grace.
One may mount to the Archiepiscopal place.
And wield the crosier, an awful thing.
The envy of all, and — the parsons' King!
O Jove! Who would struggle with learning pale.
That could beat down the world by the strength of Ale!
For me,—I avow, could my thoughtless prime
Come back with the wisdom of mournful time,
I'd labour — I'd toil — by night and day,
(Mixing liquors and books away,)
Till I conquer'd that high and proud degree,
M. A. (Master of Ale) of Trinity.

Barry Cornwall

Brasenose Ale

How Brasenose College came by its peculiar name is a much disputed point. There is a legend that in the far-off time of long ago certain students of the temporary university at Stamford, the iron ring of whose door-knocker was fitted in a nose of brass, migrated to Oxford, and there set up a brazen nose over the entrance of their college as a souvenir of their former abode.

Equally plausible is the tradition that upon the site of the college brewery once stood King Alfred's *brasinium* (brewhouse), and that the name, clinging to the place through all the changes and chances of a thousand years, now appears under the slightly modified form of Brasenose. If the latter theory be correct, the Shrovetide feast and the yearly ode in praise of Brasenose Ale may be attributed to the desire to keep green the memory of the famous brewhouse of the good King, and the mighty liquor therein brewed for the royal table.

From The Curiosities of Ale and Beer *by John Bidkerdyke (1889)*

In Praise of Brasenose Ale

Lo! Prior* hastens with his motley crew,
To pour the foaming liquor to our view:

Clasps his firm hand in all a Butler's pride
The cup no Brasenose Fellow e'er denied:

Yet secret triumph o'er his brow has cast
That Ale the sweetest, as that brew the last!

'Away, ye lighter drinks! Ye swipes, away.
Where masters bully, and where boys obey,'

The brewer cried; and taught the Ale to live
With all the charms that malt and hops could give.

Warm'd at his touch, behold the vapours rise
In all their genuine fragrance to the skies:

No beer-shops bev'rage, such as Cockneys buy.
Foul to the taste, and loathsome to the eye;

No dingy mixture, vulgarly call'd swipes;
No quassia juice, promoter of the gripes;

But true proportions of good hops and malt.
Mingled with care, then stow'd within the vault:

The hue that tells its potency—the scent
That breathes as if from blest Arabia sent.

Still o'er his Ale fond Prior hangs confest,
And joy and triumph swell his manly breast.

'RJB', (1835)

*Butler of Brasenose College, Oxford, in the mid-nineteenth century.

The Dreaded North of the Tweed

And good as Scotch strong beer is, I cannot say that the lighter and medium kinds are very good in Scotland. In fact, in Edinburgh I used to import beer of this kind from Lincolnshire, where there is no mistake about it. My own private opinion is that John Barleycorn, north of Tweed, says: 'I am for whisky, and not for ale.'

From Beer and Cider *by George Saintsbury (1845-1933)*

Inn Memoriam

'O Sir,' said Dr. Johnson, 'there is nothing which has yet been contrived by man, by which so much happiness is produced, as by a good tavern or inn.'

Boswell

Winter Warmer in August

...though it was but about the middle of August, and in some places the harvest hardly got in, we saw the mountains covered with snow, and felt the cold very acute and piercing, but we found, as in all these northern countries, the people had a happy way of mixing the warm and the cold together; for the store of good ale which flows plentifully in the most mountainous parts of this country, seems abundantly to make up for all the inclemencies of the season, or difficulties of travelling.

From A Tour Through the Whole Island of Great Britain *by Daniel Defoe (1727)*

A Bumper of Good English Ale

D'ye mind me, I once was a Sailor,
And in different countries I've been;
If I lie, may I go for a tailor.
But a thousand fine sights I have seen.

I've been crammed with good things like a wallet,
And I've guzzled more drink than a whale;
But the very best stuff to my palate
Is a glass of your English good ale.

Your doctors may boast of their lotions,
And ladies may talk of their tea,
But I envy them none of their potions,
A glass of good stingo* for me:

The doctor may sneer if he pleases,
But my recipe never will fail,
For the physic that cures all diseases
Is a bumper of English good ale.

When my trade was upon the salt ocean,
Why, there I had plenty of grog;

And I liked it, because I'd a notion
It sets one's good spirits agog:

But since upon land I've been steering
Experience has altered my tale,
For nothing on earth is so cheering,
As a bumper of English good ale.

a strong beer from Yorkshire

Anon, from The Universal Songster, (1825).

Irish Moss Ale

Irish moss ale is made in the following manner: — Take one ounce of Irish moss, one ounce of hops, one ounce of ginger, one ounce of Spanish juice, and one pound of sugar. Ten gallons of water are added and the mixture is boiled, fermented, and bottled. The consideration of the name of this liquor and the actual constituents may possibly remind readers of the old tale of that very clever person who made soup out of a stone with the assistance of a few such trifles as beef, vegetables, and flavourings.

From *The Curiosities of Ale and Beer* by John Bickerdyke (1889)

The Empty Bottle

Ah, liberty! how like thou art
To this large bottle lying here,
Which yesterday from foreign mart,
Came filled with potent English beer!
A touch of steel — a hand — a gush
A pop that sounded far and near —
A wild emotion — liquid rush —
And I had drunk that English beer!
And what remains? — An empty shell!

A lifeless form both sad and queer,
A temple where no god doth dwell —
The simple memory of beer!

William Aytoun (1813-1865)

Almighty Beer, the Fountain of All Goodness

The latter part of the sixteenth and the first half of the seventeenth centuries seem to have been remarkable for a great excess of alehouses, having regard to the wants of the population at the time. In 1591 a report of the Queen's Council on the state of Lancashire and Cheshire states that the streets and alehouses are so crowded during service time that there was none in church but the curate and his clerk; that ale-houses were innumerable, and that great abuses prevailed.

From *The Curiosities of Ale and Beer* by John Bickerdyke (1889)

Nottingham Ale

Ye bishops and deacons, priests, curates and vicars,
Come taste, and you'll certainly find it is true.
That Nottingham Ale is the best of all liquors,
And who understand the good creature like you?

It dispels every vapour, saves pen, ink, and paper;
For when you're disposed in the pulpit to rail
It will open your throats, you may preach without notes,
When inspired with full bumpers of Nottingham Ale.

'Gunthorpe', in the Westminster Magazine *(18th century)*

From The Deserted Village

Low lies that house where nut-brown draughts inspired,
Where grey-beard mirth and smiling toil retired;
Where village statesmen talked with looks profound,
And news, much older than the Ale, went round.
Obscure it sinks, nor shall it more impart
An hour's importance to a poor man's heart

Oliver Goldsmith (1730-1774)

Barley Wine

...give us some of your best barley wine, the good liquor that our honest forefathers did use to drink of; the drink which preserved their health, and made them live so long and do so many good deeds.

From The Compleat Angler *by Izaak Walton (1653)*

Bacchanalian Joys Defeated

While I'm at the Tavern quaffing
Well disposed for t'other quart.
Come's my wife to spoil my laughing,
Telling me 'tis time to part:
Words I knew, were unavailing.
Yet I sternly answered, no!
'Till from motives more prevailing,
Sitting down she treads my toe:
Such kind tokens to my thinking,
Most emphatically prove
That the joys that flow from drinking,
Are averse to those of love.
Farewell friends and t'other bottle,
Since I can no longer stay.

Love more learn'd than Aristotle,
Has, to move me, found the way.

Anon, 17th century.

The Highgate Oath

A curious custom, known as the Highgate Oath, held its ground for many a long year, and has only fallen into disuse within living memory. When a traveller passed through Highgate towards London for the first time he was brought before a pair of horns at one of the taverns*, and there a mock oath was administered to him, to the effect that he would never drink small beer when he could get strong, unless he liked it better; that, with a similar saving clause, he would never drink gruel when he could command turtle soup; nor make love to the maid, when he could court the mistress, unless he preferred the maid; with much more to the same effect.

*This is believed to have taken place at the Wrestlers, a pub in London N6, where the 'horns' can still be seen.

From *The Curiosities of Ale and Beer* by John Bickerdyke (1889)

The Fruits of Ale

The fruits of ale are unto drunkards such,
To make 'em swear and lie that drink too much.
But my ale, being drunk with moderation,
Will quench thirst and make merry recreation.

John Taylor, 'The Water Poet' (1580-1653)

His Pot is Just

His liquor's good, his pot is just,
The Landlord's poor, and cannot trust;
For he has trusted to his sorrow,
So pay to-day, he'll trust to-morrow.

Old pub sign

At Last

Long have I travelled far and near,
On purpose to find out good beer,
And at last I've found it here.

Sign at the Waggon and Horses, Brighton

Taste a Mug

Under these trees, in sunny weather,
Just try a cup of ale, however;
And if in tempest, or in storm,
A couple then to make you warm:
But when the day is very cold.
Then taste a mug a twelvemonth old.

Sign at the Rodney Pillar Inn, Creggin, Montgomeryshire

Beer at Harvest-Time

Beneath some shelt'ring heap of yellow corn
Rests the hoop'd keg, and friendly cooling horn,
That mocks alike the goblet's brittle frame,

Its costlier potions, and its nobler name.
To Mary first the brimming draught is given,
By toil made welcome as the dews of heaven,
And never lip that press'd its homely edge,
Had kinder blessings or a heartier pledge.

From The Farmer's Boy *by Robert Bloomfield (1766-1823)*

Christmas Ale

With footstep slow, in furry pall yclad,
His brows enreathed with holly never sere.
Old Christmas comes, to close the waned year,
And aye the shepherd's heart to make right glad,
Who, when his teeming flocks are homeward had,
To blazing hearth repairs, and nut-brown beer.

John Codrington Bampfylde (1754-1796/7)

Old Christmas Carol

Mye boyes come here
There's capital cheere
'Tis Christmas tyme, let myrthe goe rounde
With a flaggon of ale, by tyme well brown'd.
Drink boyes drinke
And never thinke
Of crustie old tyme, his scythe and his glasse,
He cannot, nor dare not, this waye passe.

Anon

He Who Drinks Small Beer

He who drinks small beer, goes to bed sober.
Falls as the leaves do fall, that fall in October;
He who drinks strong ale, goes to bed mellow.
Lives as he ought to live, and dies a jolly fellow.

Old drinking song

Can this be Porter?

And what this flood of deeper brown,
Which a white foam does also crown,
Less white than snow, more white than mortar?
Oh, my soul! Can this be Porter?

Anon

Porter

Harwood*, my townsman, he invented first
Porter to rival wine, and quench the thirst:
Porter, which spreads its fame half the world o'er,
Whose reputation rises more and more;
As long as Porter shall preserve its fame,
Let all with gratitude our Parish name.

From The Gentleman's Magazine, *1819*

*Ralph Harwood, said to be the first brewer of Porter around 1730

When to Old England I Came Home

When to Old England I came home,
What joy to see the tankard foam
When treading London's well-known ground,

If e'er I feel my spirits tire,
I haul my sail and look up around
In search of Whitbread's best entire.
I spy the name of Calvert,
Of Curtis, Cox, and Co.;
I give a cheer and bawl for't,
Again I hope before I die,
Of England's can the taste to try;
For many a league I'd go about
To take a draught of Gifford's stout;
I spy the name of Truman,
Of Maddox, Meux, and Co.;
The sight makes me a new man,
'A pot of porter, ho!'
When to Old England I come home,
What joy to see the tankard foam!
With heart so light and frolic high,
I drink it off to liberty.

Anon (1800)

Beer and Skittles

Life isn't all beer and skittles—but beer and skittles, or something better of the same sort, must form a good part of every Englishman's education.

From Tom Brown's Schooldays *by Thomas Hughes (1857)*

Nut-Brown Ale

Where love of wealth and rusty coin prevail,
What hopes of sugar'd cakes or nut-brown ale?

William King

Old English Beer

What is it that makes an Englishman brave,
Sooner than spirits that send to the grave?
Barley drink divine!
Better than all your meagre wine,
Weakening stuff your poor thin wine,
Then fill up a cup with hearty cheer,
There's nothing like beer the heart to cheer.
No! Ambrosia fine 'tis good as wine,
Clear, strong and richer than good wine
Hurrah! Nothing like beer, like old English beer, hurrah!

Anon, from In Praise of Ale *(1886)*

Old Christmas Carol

Come, help us to raise
Loud songs to the praise
Of good old England pleasures:
To the Christmas cheer,
And the foaming Beer.
And the buttery's solid treasures.

Anon

The Barley Mow

Here's a health to the barley-mow, my brave boys.
Here's a health to the barley-mow!
We'll drink it out of the jolly brown bowl.
Here's a health to the barley-mow!

Chorus: — Here's a health to the barley-mow, my brave boys
Here's a health to the barley-mow !
We'll drink it out of the nipperkin*, boys.

and so it proceeds, 'quarter-pint,' 'half-pint,' 'pint,' 'quart,' 'pottle,' 'gallon,' 'half-anker,' 'anker,' 'half-hogshead,' 'hogshead,' 'pipe,' 'well,' 'river,' 'ocean,' always in the third line repeating the whole of the previously-named measures backwards.

From *The Curiosities of Ale and Beer* by John Bickerdyke (1889)

The Beer Drinking Briton

Come join, honest Britons, in chorus with me.
Let us sing our own treasures, old England's good cheer,
The profits and pleasures of stout British beer.
Your wine-tippling, dram-sipping fellows retreat.
But your beer-drinking Britons can never be beat.

The French, with their vineyards, are meagre and pale,
They drink of the squeezings of half-ripened fruit;
But we, who have hop-grounds to mellow our ale,
Are rosy and plump and have freedom to boot.

Anon, from the Literary Magazine *1757*

Tea-Total

The drink which has come to supply the place of beer has, in general, been tea. It is notorious that tea has no useful strength in it; that it contains nothing nutritious; that it, besides being good for nothing, has badness in it, because it is well known to produce want of sleep in many cases, and in all cases, to shake and weaken the nerves. It is, in fact, a weaker kind of laudanum, which enlivens for the moment and deadens afterwards. At any rate it communicates no strength to the body; it does not, in any degree, assist in affording what labour demands.

William Cobbett, Cottage Economy *(1822)*

A Glass of Old English Ale

They talk about their foreign wines — Champagne and bright Moselle,
And think because they're from abroad that we must like them well.
And of their wholesome qualities they tell a wondrous tale;
But sour or sweet they cannot beat a glass of old English ale.

Chorus
So come what will, boys, drink it still
Your cheeks will never pale.
Their foreign stuff is well enough,
But give me old English ale,
My boys.
But give me old English ale.

When schoolboy friends meet once again, who have not met for years.
Say, over what will they sit down and talk of their careers?
Your 'wishy-washy' wines won't do, and fiery spirits fail.
For nothing blends the hearts of friends like good old English ale.

Chorus. So come what will, etc.

Dy'e think my eye would be as bright, my heart as light and gay,
If I and 'old John Barleycorn' did not shake hands each day?
No, no; and though teetotallers at malt and hops may rail.
At them I'll laugh and gaily quaff my glass of old English ale.

Chorus. So come what will, etc.

J. Caxton, from In Praise of Ale *(1888)*

Brasenose Ale

Brown as the nut, yet crystal as the wave
Where Delphian maids their sweeping tresses lave;
What more than mortal drink, or human cheer.
Stands like the beverage of some by-gone year?

See, big with Ale, with liquor that defies
The tap of Whitbread, and Guinness outvies;
Conscious of giant strength, as if it knew
The gods themselves would bless them at the view —
The tankard stands; though mild, awakens still
Freshman's mute gaze, and Fellow's rapt'rous thrill;
And proud that Oxford sports no better malt.
It quits the gloomy regions of the vault.
Lo! Prior hastens with his motley crew,
To pour the foaming liquor to our view:
Clasps his firm hand in all a Butler's pride
The cup no Brasenose Fellow e'er denied:
Yet secret triumph o'er his brow has cast
That Ale the sweetest, as that brew the last!

G. W. Latham

Of True British Growth is the Nectar we Boast

Of true British growth is the nectar we boast,
The homely companion of plain boil'd and roast,
Yet suited for Hall or for Parlour.
Whenever with friends we're inclined to be merry,
'Tis better to give honest Ale than bad Sherry,
Or hope to deceive with Marsala.

Anon

Beef and Ale

Beef and ale like this our yeomen
Ate and drank, those famous bowmen
Who dealt death among our foemen
Fighting at Creci.

M. Macmillan

Last Orders

Call frequently.
Drink moderately,
Pay honourably.
Be good company,
Part friendly,
Go home quietly.

Old pub sign,
Sittingbourne, Kent.

Other books from Montpelier Publishing
Available from Amazon

The Pipe Smoker's Companion

The Slow Bicycle Companion

The Cigar Collection

The Frugal Gentleman

Advice to Gentlemen

The Men's Guide to Frugal Grooming

How to Make Wine Quickly, Cheaply and Easily

A Treasury of Thrift

Marriage Advice

Wedding Jokes

After Dinner Laughs

The Simple Living Companion

Printed in Great Britain
by Amazon